WHEN DARWIN SAILED
the Sea

WHEN DARWIN SAILED

the Sea

DAVID LONG

SAM KALDA

WIDE EYED EDITIONS

CONTENTS

TO THE MOTHER I NEVER KNEW.

~ D.L.

TO MY DAD, A MAD SCIENTIST.

~ S.K.

WHO WAS CHARLES DARWIN?

"FALSE FACTS ARE HIGHLY INJURIOUS TO THE PROGRESS OF SCIENCE."

Charles Robert Darwin began his academic career as a struggling student with average grades and a tendency to avoid lectures. But this was just the beginning of a long and influential career that would see Darwin make one of the single most important discoveries of all time and go on to become one of the greatest and most famous scientists in history.

Darwin was born in 1809 and grew up in a large, comfortable house in Shropshire. His father Robert Darwin was a successful doctor, and his mother Susannah Darwin looked after Charles and his five siblings. The children spent their time playing outside, and young Charles learnt how to fish and ride ponies. However, when Darwin was only eight years old his mother Susannah died. After that, Darwin's father spent more and more time focused on his medical practise and the running of the house was left to the children. Because of this, Darwin was mostly brought up by his three older sisters, Marianne, Caroline and Susan.

From a young age Charles disliked school. He found his lessons dull and boring and could never see the point in learning Latin or studying Greek. He quickly became fascinated by wildlife and the natural world which excited him much more than his lessons. He spent as much time as possible exploring the great outdoors, collecting sandy seashells, cracked birds' eggs,

DARWIN LATER WROTE, "I BELIEVE THAT I WAS CONSIDERED BY ALL MY MASTERS AND BY MY FATHER AS A VERY ORDINARY BOY, RATHER BELOW THE COMMON INTELLIGENCE."

fluttering moths and any other creature or plant he could lay his hands on. He even joined his brother in creating homemade chemistry experiments in their own back garden.

Despite his poor grades and clear lack of enthusiasm for education, Robert Darwin was determined that his son would make something of himself and attend university. He wanted his son to follow him into the world of medicine and when he was 16 years old Darwin's father sent him to Edinburgh University.

Both Darwin's father and grandfather studied medicine at Edinburgh University and it was considered by most to be one of the best medical schools in the country. But not by Darwin. It wasn't long after arriving at his new university that Darwin wrote to his father saying he found the lectures stupid and boring. He was horrified by the sight of blood, repulsed by his anatomy lectures and completely shocked when he saw surgeons operating on patients without using anaesthetics. These hadn't been invented yet and Darwin couldn't bear to even watch an operation, let alone take part in one.

DARWIN ENROLLED AT EDINBURGH UNIVERSITY IN 1825 WHEN HE WAS JUST 16 YEARS OLD.

DARWIN SPENT 40 HOURS LEARNING HOW TO STUFF ANIMALS.

However, one thing he did find interesting about his new life were the chemistry experiments. He soon became friends with John Edmonstone, a freed slave from Guyana who taught him how to stuff birds and animals and delighted Darwin with stories about the South American rainforest which he remembered in fascinating detail. Darwin also came to know Dr. Robert Grant who was a lecturer at the university. Grant had a passion for studying marine biology and introduced Darwin to the Plinian Society. This group was interested in natural science and it was here that, with Grant's encouragement, Darwin wrote his first ever scientific paper – about sea-shore animals. Although Darwin's first years in Edinburgh weren't academically successful, the seeds of the evolutionary thinking that he would go on to write about later had already begun to blossom...

After two years at Edinburgh Darwin returned home from Scotland but, much to his father's annoyance, he didn't have a degree. Worried that his son was becoming lazy, Robert suggested that Darwin try for another degree. This time it was decided he would study divinity (religious studies) at the University of Cambridge. Perhaps the young Darwin could become a country vicar instead of a doctor, another suitable occupation for a respectable Victorian gentleman.

Darwin preferred the atmosphere in Cambridge but, once again, he found it hard to concentrate on what he was meant to be studying. His attention drifted and he began taking long walks and exploring the countryside on horseback, accompanied by Dash, his pet dog – which he found far more enjoyable than books, essays, and lectures.

DARWIN'S FATHER ACCUSED HIM OF WASTING TIME INSTEAD OF STUDYING.

It didn't take Darwin long to discover that his real passion was not related to his new studies in divinity at all. Far more interesting were botany and geology, the studies of plants and rocks, and he began an impressive collection of beetles and insects. He became great friends with John Henslow who was a professor of botany and even attended Henslow's botany course – instead of focusing on his own academic work. It was also during his time at Cambridge that Darwin joined the infamous Glutton Club.

This was a student club where members got together once a week to cook and eat unusual things. They tried various different birds including hawk and bittern, but Darwin thought the worst thing they ever tried was a brown owl. Darwin wrote that the taste was "indescribable" and it wasn't long after this dish that the club stopped meeting.

IN LATER LIFE DARWIN TRIED MORE STRANGE DISHES INCLUDING IGUANAS, AN OSTRICH-LIKE BIRD AND A 20-POUND RODENT.

Despite his poor grades and whatever his father might have thought, Darwin was an inquisitive young man and clearly very intelligent. He was also determined not to fail again. Towards the end of his time at Cambridge he threw himself into his studies to ensure that

he would leave university with a degree this time. The effort exhausted him, but the work paid off: Darwin's exam results were so good that he came tenth out of nearly two hundred students. He had no real desire to join the church, but with a degree under his belt no one could say that Darwin had wasted his years as a student.

Darwin was not destined to become a doctor or a clergyman but nonetheless his time spent in Cambridge and Scotland had not been a complete waste. Outside of his official classes Darwin had become acquainted with important scientists, like Henslow, and had learned a huge amount about the natural world.

He was beginning to understand how different rocks were formed and how plants could be identified and classified in a systematic way. By mixing with forward-thinking tutors and other bright students he had also begun to question accepted theories and ideas rather than simply believing everything he read or was told.

Charles Darwin, in other words, had taken the first important steps towards becoming a scientist. The following years would see him start to develop his own scientific theories. He had no clue yet what these might be, but one of his ideas would turn out to be revolutionary and so exciting that it would change the way humans view the world and alter our understanding of how we, as people, came into existence.

As he prepared to leave Cambridge, all of this lay ahead of Darwin. However, unaware of what the future had in store, Darwin's only thought now was that he desperately wanted to travel. He wanted to see more of this incredible, colourful and diverse world, and to study its plants and animals as closely as he possibly could.

Chapter 2

BEAGLE SETS SAIL

"NEVER... DID A VESSEL LEAVE ENGLAND BETTER PROVIDED, OR FITTED FOR THE SERVICE SHE WAS DESTINED TO PERFORM."

Two hundred years ago, while Darwin was still a curious schoolboy collecting seashells and speckled birds' eggs in his own back garden, an important new ship was under construction on the River Thames. HMS *Beagle* was built at the Royal Navy's immense Woolwich Dockyard to the east of London. Within a few years of its launch it would change the course of Darwin's life and transform the way that scientists studied the world.

The *Beagle* was built as a warship, one of around a hundred that were constructed at the same time. In the 19th century, Britain had the most powerful navy in the world and its ships played an important role in expanding what was to become the largest empire in history.

These new 'Cherokee-class' vessels were brig-sloops, which meant that they had two masts rather than three. HMS *Beagle* was not one of the largest ships in the fleet, but was equipped with ten guns and had a crew of around 120. The guns were mostly a type called a 'carronade', which are smaller than a cannon but extremely effective in close combat.

In spite of this impressive armoury, the *Beagle* never actually fought in any sea battles. After being launched in May 1820, she took part in the Royal Navy's celebrations for the coronation of King George IV, and in July the ship became the first fully-rigged warship to sail under London Bridge in more than 600 years. But shortly afterwards, the Royal Navy decided it had no use for the *Beagle* as a fighting ship and

THE *BEAGLE* MEASURED 27 METRES LONG AND 7 METRES WIDE, AND WEIGHED 235 TONS.

for the next few years the vessel lay at anchor in the River Thames. Eventually, the decision was taken to convert the *Beagle* into a ship used for exploration and long-distance survey work – a decision that would go on to change the face of science forever.

This long-distance survey work would focus on something called hydrographic surveys. This involved the accurate measurement and recording of ocean and river currents, tides and various coastal features. Detailed knowledge of these different elements was becoming more important as Britain's empire expanded, and as navigational methods became more sophisticated. The Royal Navy needed the best possible maps (known as sea charts) and only the most accurate surveys could provide the information needed to draw them up.

ACCURATE NAVIGATION REQUIRED THE BEST, MOST UP-TO-DATE MAPS POSSIBLE.

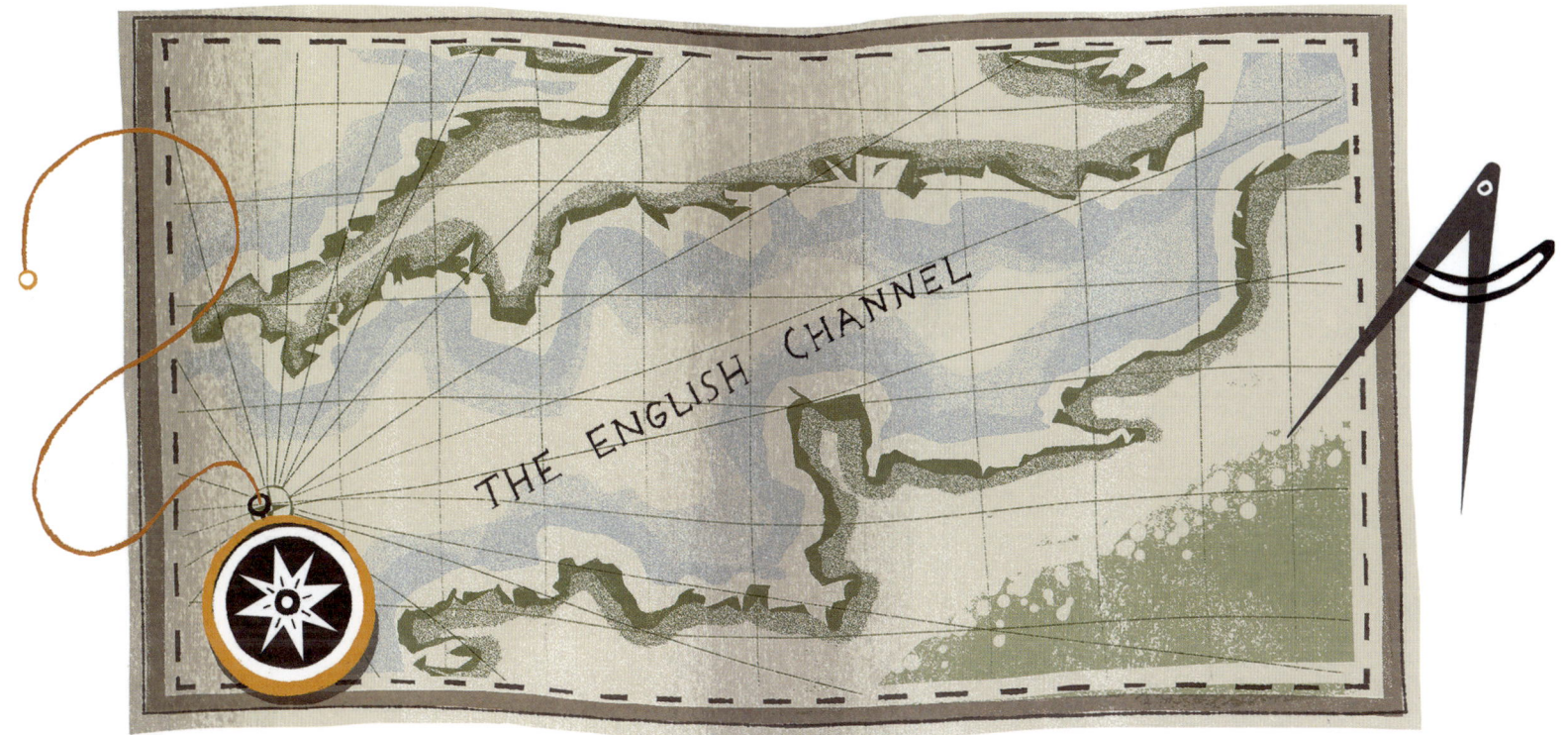

Officers in the Royal Navy were trained to carry out these surveys. In 1826 a crew of 75 men boarded the HMS *Beagle* and under the command of Captain Pringle Stokes they set sail from Plymouth to help gather this information. Together with the officers and crew of another, larger ship, the HMS *Adventure*, Captain Stokes had been ordered to produce new sea charts for the coast of South America. One of the hardest parts of this was going to be measuring and describing the confusing and often treacherous maze of channels and tiny islands at Tierra del Fuego on the remote southern tip of South America.

The ship set sail in May and had to travel thousands of miles across the stormy Atlantic just to reach South America, where their work would begin. The sailors all knew that, once they arrived, exploring a wild coastline without accurate charts would be extremely dangerous. The two ships had to sail through several narrow, rocky channels and along unknown and often fast-moving rivers. Strong and unpredictable tides, powerful storms and heavy blizzards meant that sailors' lives were constantly at risk. Dense fog and thick clouds also made it impossible to see the stars, which sailors used for accurate navigation.

After two years at sea in these terrible conditions, Captain Stokes was exhausted. He fell into a deep depression and locked himself in his cabin. For several weeks he stayed alone and isolated behind his locked door and refused to come out or to speak to any of the crew. Unable to take any more, in August 1828, Captain Stokes killed himself. Without a captain to direct the crew the decision was made to sail back to land where they could carry out repairs and restock with food and fresh water.

STOKES DESCRIBED THE SEA AS 'DREARY' AND THE SHORES AS 'INHOSPITABLE' WHICH MIGHT HAVE BEEN AN INDICATION OF HOW HE WAS FEELING.

ROBERT FITZROY JOINED THE NAVY AT THE AGE OF JUST 15.

A new captain had to be appointed before the *Beagle* could return to England. The job was given to Robert Fitzroy, an expert sailor and surveyor. He was also a keen meteorologist (someone who studies the weather) and had made a habit of observing the weather several times a day, becoming skilled at predicting what would happen to it the following night and day. He called these predictions 'forecasts' – a name we still use today – and later was considered one of the world's leading weather experts. Accurate forecasts are still vital for anyone travelling by sea, but this isn't what Robert Fitzroy is remembered for. Today he is best known for his decision to invite the young Charles Darwin to join him for a second, even longer voyage on the HMS *Beagle*.

Chapter 3

A BOTANIST COMES ABOARD

"NOTHING CAN BE MORE IMPROVING TO A YOUNG NATURALIST, THAN A JOURNEY IN A DISTANT COUNTRY."

Without lectures or troublesome timetables to hold him back, Darwin was determined to see more of the world. His first idea was to sail to the Canaries, a group of volcanic islands about 96 kilometres off the north coast of Africa. This was an extremely ambitious journey for a young man and would involve a round trip of almost 5,000 kilometres.

Darwin soon realised that this wasn't going to be achievable and so he settled for a trip to Wales instead. Once there, Darwin began studying the landscape and local geology of the area. Darwin loved his newfound freedom to finally dedicate all his time to the natural world. He found the act of collecting and identifying specimens completely fascinating and spent many hours poring over his findings and classifying them. He noted that, "Science consists in grouping facts so that general laws or conclusions may be drawn from them" – this was to prove an invaluable lesson.

Around the same time, John Henslow, the Cambridge tutor Darwin had befriended during his divinity degree, heard that HMS *Beagle* was preparing for its second voyage. Captain Fitzroy was looking for a companion, someone whose friendship and conversation might help him avoid the loneliness that had affected Pringle Stokes so badly. However, the captain wasn't interested in simply taking along a passenger. His officers and crew were perfectly capable of carrying out the hydrographic surveys, and he certainly didn't need another sailor. Instead, Captain Fitzroy felt it would be useful to have someone on the ship who could put together accurate reports about the countries he planned to visit. He wanted someone with an understanding of wildlife, botany and geology – Henslow immediately thought of Darwin.

Darwin sounded ideal. He was only 22 and relatively inexperienced, but he was keen, intelligent and available to set sail straightaway. The position onboard was an unpaid one which meant that Darwin was going to have to fund his place on the ship himself. Charles knew he would have to ask his father to pay for the journey. After a failed medical degree and a wasted education in divinity, Robert Darwin had had enough and flat-out refused to help Darwin with this new venture. Charles was crestfallen. He was desperate to undertake this new adventure, but without money, how could he secure his place on the ship? Darwin took a trip to see his uncle Josiah Wedgwood and urged him to help. This was a once in a lifetime opportunity! Much to Darwin's relief, Josiah agreed and wrote to Robert, convincing him to support Darwin's journey.

With his financial worries taken care of, Darwin met with Captain Fitzroy to discuss the impending voyage. The captain was full of admiration for the young man's knowledge and enthusiasm, but he did have one serious reservation: Charles Darwin's nose. There was a popular theory in the early 19th century that it was possible to tell a person's character and personality from their facial features. Captain Fitzroy was convinced that no one with a nose like Darwin's would have the energy or determination needed for a long sea voyage. For a while it looked like Darwin's nose was going to put an end to his dreams, and that the young man wouldn't be going anywhere. Fortunately, the captain unexpectedly changed his mind and invited him to come on board.

FITZROY BELIEVED THAT THE SHAPE OF DARWIN'S NOSE INDICATED THAT HE WOULD BE TOO WEAK FOR SUCH A LONG SEA JOURNEY.

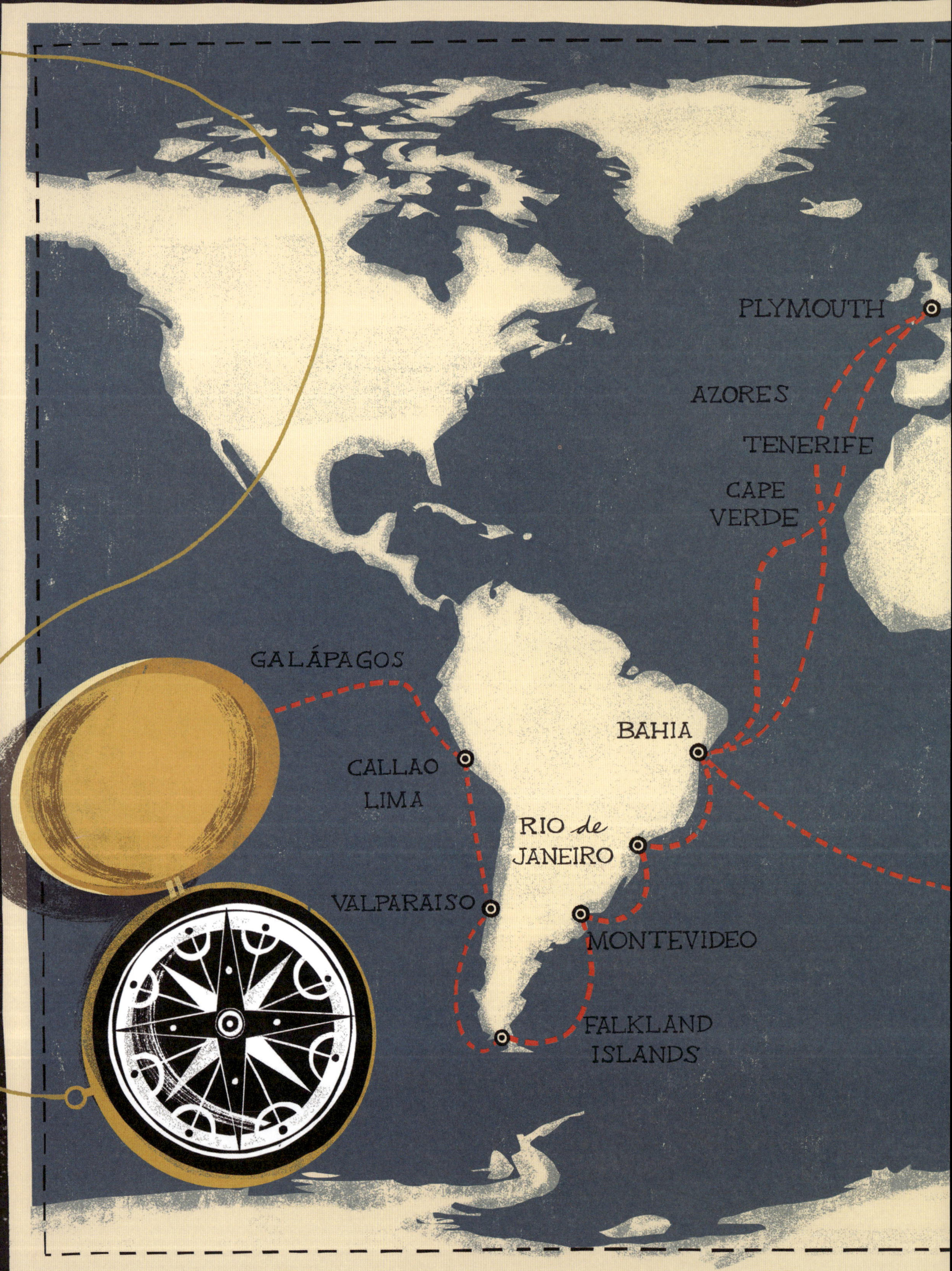

PLYMOUTH

AZORES

TENERIFE

CAPE
VERDE

GALÁPAGOS

BAHIA

CALLAO
LIMA

RIO *de*
JANEIRO

VALPARAISO

MONTEVIDEO

FALKLAND
ISLANDS

Darwin's great adventure was about to begin – finally he was going to see the world he had heard so much about from John Edmonstone. Darwin was told that the second voyage of the *Beagle* would last at least two years and would involve sailing to South America and surveying the coasts of Brazil and Argentina. The ship would then revisit Tierra del Fuego before heading to the Falkland and Galápagos Islands, Tahiti, and Port Jackson in Australia. On its way across the Atlantic, Captain Fitzroy planned to stop at several smaller islands, including the Canaries and the Cape Verde Islands which lay farther south.

COCOS
(KEELING)
ISLANDS

MAURITIUS

SYDNEY

SECOND VOYAGE
of the
BEAGLE

CAPE
TOWN

KING
GEORGE'S
SOUND

HOBART

The young naturalist was thrilled with the plan – it would mean he could begin collecting exotic new specimens within a few weeks of setting sail.

Before embarking on such a long voyage, the *Beagle* needed some repairs and modifications after its first long voyage. A lot of new scientific equipment was gathered, including a lightning conductor. This was a cutting-edge new invention designed to protect wooden vessels from catching fire if one was struck by lightning. Captain Fitzroy also ordered 22 of the most advanced marine chronometers (a special type of clock) because precise navigation required the most accurate timekeeping possible. Five new sympiesometers or barometers were also acquired. These measured changes in air pressure and would help the captain to compile his regular weather forecasts.

Finally, a request was sent to the Admiralty for a set of powerful brass guns. These would replace the iron ones that interfered with the ship's magnetic compass. Unfortunately, brass was much more expensive than iron, so this request was turned down. Captain Fitzroy wanted his voyage to go as smoothly as possible and iron cannons just wouldn't do. He gritted his teeth and ordered them anyway, agreeing to pay for them using his own money.

Darwin, meanwhile, had his own preparations to make. In addition to buying three smaller guns he asked a number of experts in Cambridge to show him the best methods for preserving plant and animal specimens. He bought a new rock hammer for collecting geological samples, a microscope and a huge supply of notebooks so he wouldn't run out. He also got a clinometer which would measure the angle and orientation of rock layers and a plankton net, which could be towed behind the *Beagle* to collect microscopic samples.

By the late autumn everything was in place and, after a delay caused by unexpectedly bad weather, the ship finally set sail. The date was 27th December 1831. The historic second voyage of HMS *Beagle* had begun, and Charles Darwin was on his way.

Chapter 4

FIVE YEARS AT SEA

"THE VOYAGE OF THE *BEAGLE* HAS BEEN BY FAR THE MOST IMPORTANT EVENT OF MY LIFE AND HAS DETERMINED MY WHOLE CAREER."

Darwin's trip of a lifetime, due to last two years, became an epic journey of nearly five years. During his travels he sailed right around the globe and saw a kaleidoscope of things that no European had ever seen before.

When he left England, the 22-year-old was a bright young university graduate who thought he might return from his voyage and maybe become a vicar. But by the time the *Beagle* returned, he was a changed man. He had survived many hair-raising adventures, had become an experienced naturalist and was considered a leading expert who was well-known in both London and Cambridge for the astonishing quality (and the sheer quantity) of the spectacular specimens he had collected and sent back to England.

During those five years the crew of the *Beagle* compiled countless accurate surveys of the waters around South America, Australia, Tasmania and New Zealand. Darwin played no part in any of this. Instead, each time the *Beagle* dropped anchor, he clambered over the side of the ship and took off on long journeys of exploration into the wilderness. Exploring new territory on foot gave him a break from the misery of seasickness, which he suffered from throughout his time on the *Beagle*. His excursions into these unknown territories were exhausting and dangerous, but Darwin pressed on. These experiences were deeply exciting for a young man with an enquiring mind and a determination to learn as much as he possibly could.

OVER THE COURSE OF FIVE YEARS DARWIN AND THE *BEAGLE* VISITED FOUR DIFFERENT CONTINENTS ACROSS THE GLOBE.

One of the things that Darwin had been looking forward to most was seeing the lush Brazilian rainforest. He could hardly believe the incredible diversity of life he found there and thought the coral islands he visited were some of "the most wonderful objects in the world". When he realised that it might be possible to write a book about these different places it made him "thrill with delight".

From the very start of the voyage Darwin kept scientific journals. Notebook after notebook was filled with detailed descriptions of fossils, sketches of creatures great and small, drawings of new and unusual plants, and countless other significant discoveries that would go on to help him with his ground-breaking research. The same pages contained many insightful observations about the strange plants and mammals that he found on these expeditions.

Darwin's handwriting was often rather untidy, but his discoveries were exactly the sort of thing people back home in Britain were hungry to hear about. His fellow scientists and ordinary readers alike were excited to hear about exotic new plants and animals. In this era of exploration, British people's imaginations were captured by all the natural wonders of the world. This enthusiasm led to Darwin's journal later becoming a bestselling book.

Darwin's adventures were filled with incredible experiences, some more pleasant than others. On one memorable occasion, he encountered a group of 'gauchos' in Argentina. Gauchos are South American cowboys, herding cattle, travelling on horseback with only the bare essentials for living. Darwin was invited to ride with them and even attempted to learn how to use the gauchos' bolas, a lasso-like rope used for catching cattle. However, Darwin was not as skilled as the gauchos and only managed to throw it around his own horse's leg!

Darwin was also bitten by a blood-sucking insect he called the Benchua as he travelled through Argentina. Some believe Darwin contracted chagas disease through these insect bites and that this was the origin of Darwin's seasickness and later stomach illnesses. But for all the excitement, adventure and sense of wonder Darwin encountered, he also uncovered a darker side to these unknown lands. During a lengthy 240-kilometre trek through Brazil, Darwin was appalled to see the cruel treatment of hardworking slaves. Darwin watched, powerless, as men, women and children were treated inhumanely by their owners.

Later, in Valdivia in southern Chile, Darwin had his first experience of a terrifying earthquake. The force of it completely destroyed a nearby town. Even though this was a great tragedy, the young scientist learned a lot from studying its effects. After the ground had stopped shaking, Darwin noticed that a whole stretch of coastline had risen up by several feet. Further earthquakes occurred a few weeks later when he was walking in the Andes mountains. After finding ancient, fossilised trees on some of the higher slopes, Darwin noticed how these looked very similar to the living trees down at sea level. Thinking about this, he began to see how mountains might rise up "slowly and by little starts" in a series of earthquakes, one after another.

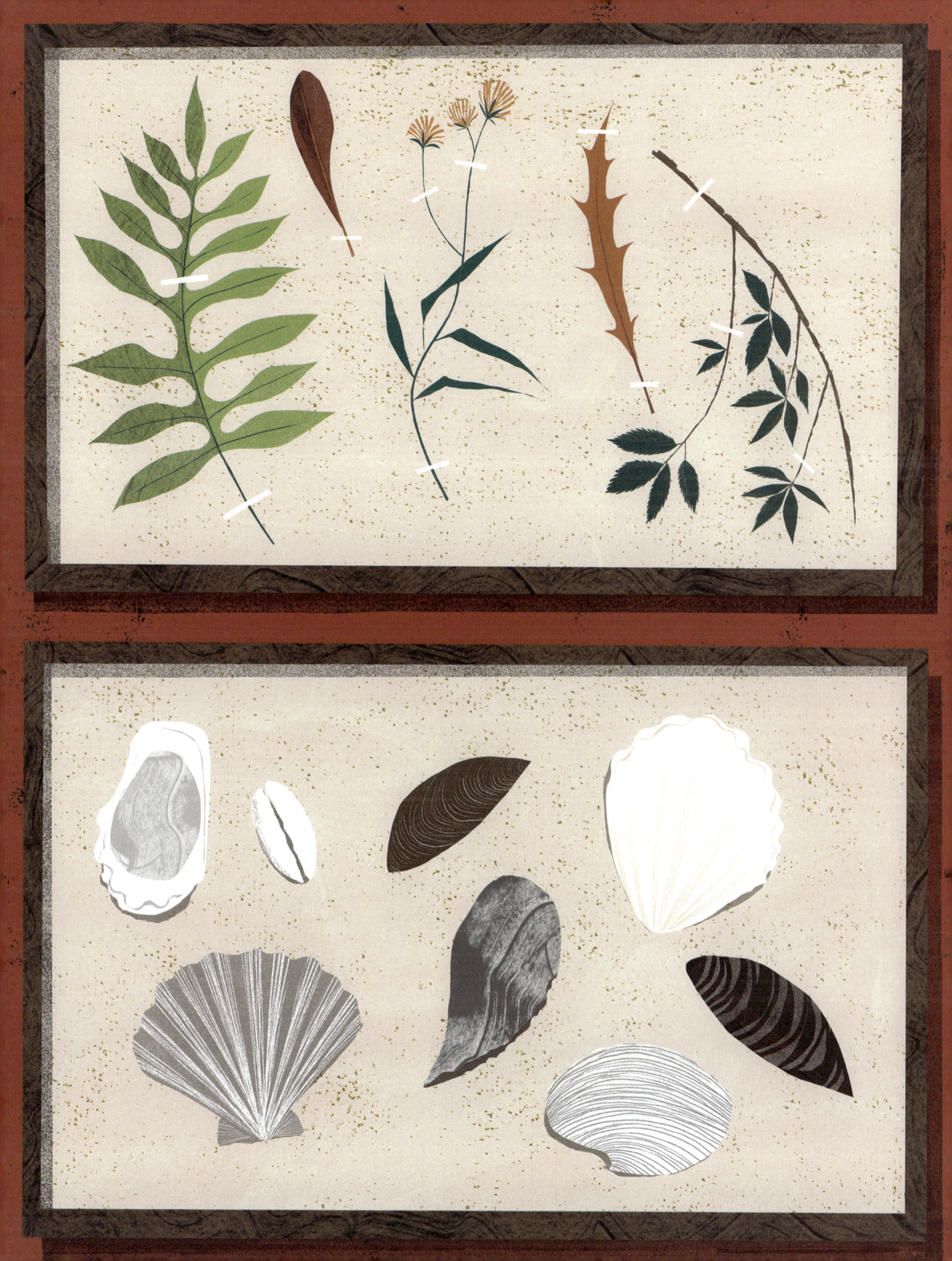

Despite the dangers, the opportunity to trek many miles through Brazil, Argentina and Chile and to explore remote island areas was an incredible gift for any young naturalist, and Darwin was determined not to waste a single moment. To him, every single day brought a new discovery, and by the end of the voyage he had collected over 1,500 different plant and animal specimens. It was an unprecedented collection and hundreds of the species were ones that had never been seen before by anyone in Europe, including other scientists.

Darwin was particularly fascinated by the way in which species he found on islands often differed from the plants and animals he found on the South American mainland. In the Falklands and the Galápagos, for example, there were plants, birds and tortoises that were completely unique to those islands and couldn't be found anywhere on the mainland. Similarly, in Australia he was struck by how many mammals there were that had never been seen anywhere else in the world. This fact lodged in Darwin's mind, and he spent many hours trying to understand what it could mean.

His trip had been marvellous, but by the spring of 1836 Darwin had something else on his mind: England. By now, Darwin was not just seasick but also homesick. The voyage had given him the knowledge and the working methods he needed for his future scientific career, but he had had enough. In fact, he was so homesick that he said that although the large island of Mauritius was really beautiful, he thought it looked best from the back of a ship that was sailing away as fast as possible.

WHILE IN MAURITIUS DARWIN WROTE TO HIS SISTER SAYING, "WE ARE ALL UTTERLY HOMESICK".

Now 27 years old, he was desperate to get back to England but Captain Fitzroy insisted they make one final detour back to South America to take a few more measurements. Five years earlier he could not have been more enthusiastic, but now he said he hated "the sea and all ships which sail on it".

Fortunately, the captain's measurements did not take long to complete and by September the *Beagle* was at last homeward bound for England. In October, five years after they had set sail, the HMS *Beagle* reached Cornwall. Darwin could not have been happier.

Chapter 5

GALÁPAGOS

"A LITTLE WORLD WITHIN ITSELF."

Once home, Darwin settled down to think and write about what he had seen on his incredible five-year voyage. He had visited so many fascinating places during the time he spent onboard the *Beagle*, but nowhere was as interesting to him or as important to the progress of science as the Galápagos Islands. Now that he was back in England he dedicated most of his time to thinking about the islands and what he had seen.

The Galapagos are a small group of islands, or an 'archipelago', situated in the Pacific Ocean, nearly 1,000 kilometres off the coast of Ecuador. The 21 islands range from just over one square kilometre to more than 4,000 square kilometres. In 1535, a Spanish bishop landed on one of the islands when his ship drifted off course, but the islands' remote location close to the equator meant that few other Europeans had ever visited them before the *Beagle* arrived 300 years later.

Because of this, most Europeans had never even heard of the Galápagos and the scientists who had heard of them knew almost nothing about the geology or wildlife found there. This is why Darwin was so eager to study them and why he leapt at the chance to explore these strange and unknown islands.

DARWIN'S SEVERE SEASICKNESS
MEANT THAT HE WAS ALWAYS
HAPPIER ON LAND.

The islands are volcanic in origin, like the Canaries, and around four million years old. This is actually quite young in geological terms (some of the islands are even still forming today) and it meant Darwin would have the opportunity to explore an active volcano for the first time. However, the islands' unique wildlife turned out to be even more inspiring than the volcano. The plants and animals Charles came across there made the greatest impact on him, and although he didn't know it at the time, it was these discoveries that would most significantly change the course of his life – and of science.

Darwin wrote in his diary that, even before landing on the first island, "the bay swarmed with animals; fish, shark and turtles were popping their heads up in all parts". Once on land he began to spot countless different species which neither he nor any other scientist had ever seen before.

The species here were nothing like the ones he had seen in South America. Among the creatures he saw were strange birds, fish, insects, snails and giant tortoises. On the black lava rocks above one beach he saw iguanas which he described as "the most disgusting, clumsy lizards". During his time there Darwin began selecting the best examples to add to his growing collection. He could then study these very closely, using the islands as a sort of giant living laboratory.

GIANT TORTOISES, LIKE THE ONES DARWIN SAW, CAN LIVE FOR OVER A HUNDRED YEARS.

The enormous tortoises that roamed the island were the most exotic and unusual animals that Darwin came across, although sadly hundreds of them had already been caught, killed and eaten by sailors from passing ships. The largest males weighed three or four times as much as a man, but one crew killed so many of them (possibly around 700) that within ten years of the *Beagle's* visit that particular species was extinct.

During his time on the Galápagos Darwin met an Englishman called Nicholas Lawson who was in charge of an Ecuadorian prison. Lawson explained to Darwin that it was possible to tell which island a tortoise came from just by looking at its shell, which Darwin found completely fascinating. Until that moment he had assumed that the wildlife would be the same on all the different islands.

IT TOOK YEARS FOR DARWIN TO REALISE THE IMPORTANCE OF SOME OF HIS DISCOVERIES.

When Darwin took a closer look at the tortoises he realised that his fellow Englishman was indeed correct. And it wasn't just the tortoises that differed from one island to the next. Studying his own specimens, Darwin could see that the varieties of plants and animals living on each of the individual islands were all slightly different. This was a hugely important discovery for Darwin. Just as the islands were all slightly different from each other – some were dry and rocky, others had more rainfall and better soil – so too were the creatures that lived on them and the vegetation that grew there.

Like the tortoise shells, the appearance of bird and plant species (and even snails) changed slightly as he moved from one island to another. Darwin wasn't sure yet why this was, but he felt sure it was important and was determined to find a reason for it. In fact, it was so significant that, although he was only in the Galápagos for five weeks, Darwin's visit to these remote islands was to have a great and lasting effect on him. Not just on the way he personally thought and wrote about nature and natural history, but on the whole course of science from that point onwards.

Darwin would eventually use the specimens he collected from the islands to illustrate and explain an exciting new scientific theory. This theory would dramatically enhance his reputation as a scientist, and completely alter the way people looked at the world. It would also mean that, instead of being somewhere most people had never heard of, the Galápagos Islands would eventually become famous as a place of enormous scientific importance and discovery.

Chapter 6

DARWIN AT HIS DESK

"A MAN WHO DARES TO WASTE ONE HOUR OF TIME HAS NOT DISCOVERED THE VALUE OF LIFE."

Once back in England, Darwin and Captain Fitzroy published a series of books based on the notes they collected in their journals. Readers were thrilled by the adventures and incredible experiences had by the explorers, and the books were a hit, making both Darwin and Fitzroy famous.

The captain soon set off on another, even longer voyage on HMS *Beagle*, although not before being awarded a prestigious gold medal by the Royal Geographical Society. Darwin, meanwhile, settled down to the long task of identifying and classifying all the different specimens he'd returned home with. After spending a short period back in Cambridge, Darwin moved to London so that he could be closer to the latest developments in science and natural history. Initially, Darwin stayed with his brother Erasmus and later moved to a house on Gower Street, which is now the site of University College London. Today there is a blue plaque commemorating his time there – near the university's Darwin Building.

Darwin also began receiving dozens of letters inviting him to make speeches about his time on HMS *Beagle* and about his incredibly exciting discoveries. Darwin accepted these invitations and toured the country giving countless talks to different scientific societies. Darwin, still only in his late twenties, was living in a world rich with scientific and free-thinking excitement. But while these speeches were enjoyable and a great success, he knew that cataloguing the collection was far more important. He wanted to get started on this as soon as possible and to follow through with his plans to donate his birds and animals to the new Zoological Society of London.

Darwin soon realised that the job of classifying such a large number of rare and unknown species was too much for one person, so he asked several other scientists to help him with this work. These included friends from his days as a student in Cambridge as well as the fossil specialist Richard Owen, inventor of the term 'dinosaur', meaning 'terrible lizard'. Owen was a highly respected naturalist and played a key role in founding the Natural History Museum, in South Kensington. He believed that everyone should be able to view biological specimens and the Natural History Museum provided everybody the opportunity to see all sorts of natural wonders.

Darwin also asked John Gould, a highly respected ornithologist (bird expert) to help him with this task. Studying the bird specimens closely, Gould managed to identify 12 different species of finch. Each species was slightly different from the last, but all of them were from the Galápagos Islands and Darwin's notes helped Gould work out which birds came from which island. It was the same when he looked at the mockingbirds Darwin had brought back (they are called this because they sometimes copy the songs of other birds). Different islands seemed to produce different species, something Gould had never seen before.

This was exactly what Darwin wanted to hear. It was this fact that had so intrigued Darwin while he was travelling. During the five years he spent sailing around the world he had been amazed by the incredible variety of plants and animals, but he had also become deeply confused.

Many of the fossils he had collected on the voyage were the remains of animals that no longer existed. Other specimens were of living creatures. But these weren't the same as the dead and fossilised ones, the ones that had lived in the past. He couldn't explain this, or why a tiny place like Galápagos had ten or eleven different kinds of tortoise when a vast area like California had only one...

IDEAS BEGAN TO FORM IN DARWIN'S MIND THAT WERE GENUINELY REVOLUTIONARY.

Darwin was beginning to wonder, like Robert Grant had before him, whether it was possible for species to change over time. If it was, it might even be possible for an entirely new species to develop that hadn't existed before. In the 19th century this was an extraordinary idea and one that most people had never considered.

DARWIN'S FINDINGS SEEMED TO SUGGEST THE BIBLE MIGHT NOT BE TRUE.

For hundreds of years most people had believed in 'creationism', which they learned from reading the Bible. This was the idea that everything on Earth had been created by God in just six days. People believed that everything they saw around them was just as God had made it. This meant that plants and animals couldn't change over time – that everything in the world was exactly as it had been when God put it there.

Darwin's discoveries suggested that this wasn't exactly true: some species did seem to be changing. Those of his fossils that didn't match any creature alive today (and the sad story of the giant tortoises which had been killed and eaten) proved that it was, in fact, possible for an entire species to go extinct and vanish forever. And as Darwin mulled over his new discovery he began to think that the opposite might also be possible: perhaps, over time, a new species could somehow appear.

Darwin had noticed something else very interesting during his expeditions from the *Beagle*. Although individual plants and animals in a species all looked very similar to each other, they were not exactly the same. He found that, instead of being perfect copies of each other, there were differences between them. He called these differences 'variations'.

These variations could be quite small. The Galápagos finches, for example, looked a lot like each other except for their beaks. These differed depending on which island they came from. Darwin had seen for himself how the different types of beak were suited to eating the different seeds or insects that each bird found on its own island. And then, later, John Gould had confirmed that there were differences between the mockingbirds from four of the different islands. Like the finches, these appeared to have changed by adapting to suit the conditions in which they lived. If this was true, then it showed that species could change or 'evolve'.

Darwin felt he had evidence that this was happening, but he didn't yet have an explanation for why it was happening. It was an exciting thought, but a frightening one, too. He knew that if he could give a scientific explanation for how and why species were changing, it would make some people incredibly angry and upset many more because it suggested that something in the Bible wasn't true. This was never his intention, but as a scientist he was determined to find out the truth.

Although Darwin spent much of his time collecting evidence that suggested species could evolve, he also spent many years after his return to England working on a range of other projects. Alongside his evolutionary research, Darwin studied barnacles and coral reefs. He also married Emma Wedgwood, started a family and moved to Down House in Kent. Unfortunately, he suffered from numerous illnesses during this time. All the while, though, Darwin continued to work on what he called his essay; developing a radical new idea that would revolutionise natural history and society.

Chapter 7

NATURAL SELECTION

"THE SURVIVAL OF THE FITTEST."

At the time that Darwin was making his evolutionary discoveries, many people believed that the story about Noah's Ark and the Great Flood in the Bible could be used to explain why certain animals, such as dinosaurs, had become extinct. What no one could explain was where new species came from.

According to the Bible, all the world's plants and animals (including humans) were created by God – something people had believed for thousands of years. It was impossible to prove this theory scientifically, but that wasn't the only difficulty. According to the Bible, God created the universe and everything in it in six days. But Darwin had discovered many living plants and creatures that weren't like the ones that he knew existed millions of years ago. His newly discovered creatures weren't around at the same time as the dinosaurs – so where did they come from?

From Darwin's discoveries it looked like new species were still being created, but no one could explain how this was happening. It certainly wasn't explained in the Bible. As a student Darwin had learned to question traditional ideas rather than just accepting them, and his new discoveries made it impossible for him to believe the story of creation that was written in the Bible.

Darwin began to think that if species changed very slowly over time then it might be possible for a new species to emerge in this way. He knew that the changes didn't occur during one single lifetime of an individual plant or animal. Instead he thought that as one generation replaced another, small variations would start to appear.

SPECIES COULD GO EXTINCT, AND OTHER NEW ONES COULD APPEAR.

A new species would emerge only after a sufficient number of generations had been born and died, allowing these small variations to alter the way a particular plant or animal looked or behaved.

To begin with, this was just an idea and not a scientific theory because Darwin couldn't describe how these variations occurred or why species were changing. It took him a while to think of a process that could explain it, but eventually he did, and he called the process 'natural selection'.

Using natural selection, Darwin was able to show why plants and animals differ so much from one country to another – or, as he had seen for himself, from one island to the next. It also enabled him to explain why some species die out (and become fossils) and why others survive.

The key thing, he realised, was the way in which plants and animals change or adapt to suit their particular environment. Some adapt very well but others don't.

The creatures that adapt well go on to breed successfully and the offspring they have are as well adapted to the environment as their parents. They thrive too and produce lots of offspring of their own. Species like this that adapt well to their environment go on to do well. Those that don't adapt suffer instead of thriving. They struggle to survive and may die without producing any young at all. Any they do produce will be poorly adapted (like their parents) and won't thrive. If this happens often enough, over time these poorly adapted species will eventually die out and become extinct.

Darwin had seen this for himself in the Galápagos. Finches with the right beaks managed to get more food which enabled them to grow larger and stronger and breed more. The female birds laid more eggs which hatched into stronger and healthier chicks. The opposite was true of birds with the wrong beaks. They weren't able to eat properly, the females laid fewer eggs, and produced fewer, weaker offspring – or, in some cases, none at all.

This process became known as 'the survival of the fittest'. This is not a phrase Darwin used when he first explained his theory, but it helps us understand the way in which the healthiest, best adapted species out-perform the others. As parents produce offspring similar to themselves, the variations that help a species survive pass from one generation to the next. The variations that don't help eventually die out.

THE MOST HELPFUL ADAPTATIONS WERE PASSED ON TO THE NEXT GENERATION.

As an example of nature selecting the best species for a particular environment, imagine a group of rabbits living in an ordinary field.

NATURAL SELECTION HAPPENS AMONG ALL SPECIES OF PLANTS AND ANIMALS, INCLUDING HUMANS.

Some of the rabbits are brown while some are white. A hungry hawk flying over the field looking for something to eat finds it much easier to spot the white rabbits. Because of this, more white rabbits are killed and eaten than brown ones. As more brown rabbits survive, more of them will go on to breed and to produce even more brown rabbits.

Brown rabbits will gradually begin to outnumber the white ones. The white rabbits could even disappear altogether. They make lovely pets (and a useful prop for a magician) but white fur is not a good adaptation in this particular environment. In this big open field, brown is a better adaptation because it provides camouflage for the rabbits. However, in a different environment (the snow-covered Arctic for example), the opposite would be true: in a snowy landscape, white rabbits would be better camouflaged than brown ones.

Darwin was beginning to realise that natural selection worked with all species, meaning plants and animals. Scientists and interested readers began to understand that this meant it applied to humans as well as wildlife. The implications of this were especially controversial.

Chapter 8

THE MOST FAMOUS SCIENTIST *in the* WORLD

"ONE LONG ARGUMENT."

It took quite some time for Darwin to work out all the details, but 20 years after his momentous voyage around the world he was ready to share his ideas with the world and published his theory of natural selection in a book he called *On the Origin of Species*.

DARWIN'S BOOK WAS AN IMMEDIATE BESTSELLER. EVERYBODY WANTED TO READ IT.

To support the theory, he included all the evidence he had gathered from the Galápagos Islands and from the other countries that he visited during his journey. The book also described the results of his own research back in England, and incorporated information and ideas he had discussed with other leading naturalists.

The publication went on sale in November 1859 and caused an immediate sensation, with the first edition selling out almost straightaway (which was very unusual for a scientific work). More copies were printed as quickly as possible – nearly three times as many as the first batch. One library ordered an incredible 500 copies, which meant that the book could be read by thousands of ordinary people who couldn't afford their own copies. A single copy cost fifteen shillings (75p) which doesn't sound like much, but in the 1850s it was more than two

weeks' wages for a lot of people. Darwin wanted as many people as possible to read his book, so he arranged for the price to be halved when it was reprinted again. New editions were published in America and in several foreign languages and these quickly sold out too.

On the Origin of Species made Darwin even more famous than he had been before, and for a while he was probably the most famous scientist anywhere in the world. But the reviews flooding in weren't always positive. His revolutionary ideas upset many readers, including some of his fellow academics. Both William Herschel, a widely respected

DARWIN'S BOOK INFURIATED MANY PEOPLE WHO READ IT, ESPECIALLY THOSE WHO WERE RELIGIOUS.

astronomer of the time, and Wilfred Owen were highly unimpressed by Darwin's theory. In Britain and abroad, religious leaders were outraged by Darwin's theory, stating that his writings were highly blasphemous (which means they disagreed with the Bible).

Most people at the time believed that we are all descended from Adam and Eve, like it says in the Bible, and Darwin's theory showed that this wasn't true. His research also proved that humans were closely related to apes and monkeys. People thought monkeys were unintelligent, dirty creatures and thought that the suggestion that humans had evolved from apes in the same way that new species of plants and animals evolved from ancient ones was completely outrageous.

The idea that men, women and children were all related to ordinary animals genuinely shocked many people. If it was true it meant that humans were just another kind of animal. Some priests and churchgoers accepted that many of the stories in the Bible couldn't be taken literally; however, they could not accept that humans were not created by God. A lot of people were deeply offended by the suggestion that they had evolved from apes; they wanted to believe humans were created as something unique and special.

Many readers simply refused to accept Darwin's evidence and heated debates about his theory carried on for years. People were so outraged by his theories that for a long time, the book was actually banned from the library of his own college at Cambridge University.

Newspapers in England and France printed cruel cartoons showing the author as a chimpanzee, and there were even protests when Queen Victoria considered making him Sir Charles Darwin.

IT SEEMS INCREDIBLE THAT A SCIENTIFIC THEORY COULD UPSET SO MANY BUT EVEN NOW THERE ARE THOSE WHO THINK DARWIN WAS WRONG.

Today, there are still people who think that Darwin and his evolutionary idea are wrong and who dismiss his ideas completely. However, most people now agree with Darwin's theories and that *On the Origin of Species* contains one of the greatest scientific discoveries of all time. Since 1859 millions of copies have been printed around the world, although no one knows exactly how many.

Although *On the Origin of Species* is Darwin's most famous and important book, he wrote many other works afterwards. His book *The Descent of Man* was published in 1871 and in this title Darwin continued to explore evolution and looked more closely at human evolution in particular. Some of his work also included studying the evolutionary reasons for the expression of emotion in humans and animals. This book included many drawings and photographs of animals and humans making facial expressions. Photography was still a brand-new technology at the time, and Darwin's use of photographs in this book was extremely innovative.

DARWIN WROTE MANY MORE IMPORTANT BOOKS ABOUT EVOLUTION.

Although some of Darwin's later theories were not as influential as his most important one, the theory of natural selection, his work remains hugely important today. One of the reasons his work is so significant is because it was the start of the long-running battle of science versus religion. But the main reason for his importance is that the author achieved two big things. Both are still relevant more than a century and a half later, and both continue to have a major influence on modern science.

MODERN RESEARCH SHOWS THAT DARWIN WAS RIGHT.

The first big thing Darwin did was to produce evidence that evolution has taken place. The second was to devise a remarkable theory that explained how evolution actually works. By demonstrating the way it affects every living thing, including humans, Darwin proved that natural selection is the key to understanding biology and the amazing diversity of life on Earth.

This disappointed and dismayed many people who wanted to believe the Bible, but modern research has shown that Darwin was right. It also upset scientists who were committed to different ideas of creation – or wished to keep humans distant from animals. Darwin's brilliant observations made humans aware for the very first time of their place in the natural world. His work also showed how scientific research and the systematic collection of evidence is crucial to our understanding of our planet and the incredible mysteries of life.

Chapter 9

DARWIN'S LEGACY

"THE TORCH THAT ILLUMINATES THE WORLD."

Charles Darwin never did become Sir Charles. In 1882 he died in his home at Down House and his family intended to bury him there. But when news spread of his death it was soon decided that Darwin deserved to be laid to rest in the magnificent Westminster Abbey in the heart of London. During the whole of the 19th century, only four other people were buried in the abbey who weren't members of the Royal Family, so this was an incredible honour.

THE FAILED MEDICAL STUDENT IS NOW CONSIDERED ONE OF THE GREATEST SCIENTISTS OF ALL TIME.

This act showed what a great scientist the failed medical student had become, and it recognised the enormous contributions that Darwin made to our understanding of the natural world. It is also significant that his coffin was carried into the abbey by some of the most important scientists working in Victorian Britain, including Alfred Russel Wallace and Joseph Hooker.

It is hard to imagine now, but when Darwin was born even scientists believed that God had created the universe (and everything in it) just a few thousand years ago. We now know our planet is more than four billion years old, but when he first climbed aboard HMS *Beagle*, Darwin didn't. He still believed much of what was said in the Bible.

As a young man he had been studying to become a priest and science was his hobby. It was only after seeing and experiencing so many new and strange things on that long and extraordinary journey that Darwin began to question the world around him. The amazing and unique species that he found on the Galápagos, he discovered, could not have been

specially created for each island. They must have evolved from similar ancestors that originated on the mainland of South America before washing up on the islands.

It took him years to work out how this evolution had occurred. At first even he did not grasp the significance of what he had seen, but today it is almost impossible to overstate the importance of what he achieved. More than a century and a half later, Darwin's theory of natural selection informs a whole range of scientific research, including genetics and medicine. And scientists around the world still believe that Darwin's theory of natural selection is one of the greatest ideas that the human mind has ever produced.

In one giant leap, Darwin's discoveries and his insights transformed human understanding of the world, and of our place in it. At the same time his meticulous, methodical work (both during the voyage and in the decades following his return home) underlined the vital importance of science and research. As a young man Darwin may have disappointed his father by his failure to become a doctor or a priest, but by the end of his life he had set a new course which no future scientist could ignore.

Chapter 10

WHAT BECAME of the BEAGLE ?

Captain Fitzroy and HMS *Beagle* returned from their third and final voyage in 1843. The Royal Navy no longer had any use for an old ship, even one as historic and as scientifically important as the *Beagle*.

The wooden hull was stripped of its guns and masts and handed over to the Board of Customs. The vessel was then renamed *Watch Vessel No. 7* and moored in the middle of a cold, bleak stretch of saltmarsh on the Essex coast. For the next few years, the former warship was no more than a lonely look-out post for the men of the Coastguard in their long battle against smugglers.

THE *BEAGLE* MADE OTHER VOYAGES WITHOUT DARWIN BUT WILL FOREVER BE ASSOCIATED WITH HIS NAME.

By 1870 the vessel that had been made so famous by Charles Darwin was too rundown even for this. Most of the remains were sold for scrap and hauled off to be broken up. Today, 200 years after *Beagle* first set sail, just a few sad fragments of wood and metal lie rotting in the mud. Only the anchor has been saved.

DARWIN'S DISCOVERIES

Darwin was an avid collector and on his incredible voyages he collected new, never-before-seen specimens that would go on to advance scientific discovery. Here is just a small collection of some of the amazing discoveries Darwin made during his work.

GIANT GROUND SLOTH

Darwin found fossils from four different types of ground sloths. Before going extinct these were some of the largest mammals that had ever lived. Their remains are now in London's Natural History Museum.

RHEA

Meals on board the *Beagle* depended on the crew catching animals to eat. Unfortunately, this included rare species and during one meal in Patagonia Darwin realised he was eating an entirely new type of bird. The Lesser Rhea was a bit like an ostrich. Fortunately, he managed to save the head, neck and wings – and some feathers!

GIANT TORTOISES

Darwin had never seen a giant tortoise before reaching the Galápagos and was surprised by the idea that it was possible to identify which island a tortoise came from just by looking at its shell. He soon proved that this was true and began looking at other types of animal to see if they too varied from island to island.

MOCKINGBIRDS

Noticing how mockingbirds from the island of San Cristóbal were unlike the mockingbirds on Floreana gave Darwin another important indication that animals gradually adapted to their environments.

FINCHES

This idea became even clearer when he discovered about a dozen previously unknown species of finch. Darwin noticed that the birds had different beaks depending on which island they came from. He realised the beaks were adapted to suit the food each bird found on its own island.

PLANTS

Darwin had a lifelong interest in botany and collected more than 200 plant species while he was in the Galápagos Islands. More than half of these turned out to grow nowhere else in the world, and Darwin identified 78 of them as entirely new species.

GLYPTODON

Darwin collected many fossils during his travels. Examples from extinct species like the glyptodon (a sort of gigantic armadillo) helped him see that animals and plants gradually changed over millions of years.

GOMPHOTHERE

The gomphothere had a trunk like a modern elephant. Some species had four tusks, others just two. They lived more than 30 million years ago but went extinct around 10,000 years ago, possibly as a result of climate change.

DARWIN'S PEOPLE

A host of fascinating characters appeared in Darwin's past and helped shape his great mind, offered him support, encouraged him to tell the world his discoveries or indeed in some cases, criticised his findings. Often left out of history books or forgotten about entirely, below are some of the incredible people who helped Darwin on his path to becoming a ground-breaking scientist.

ELIZABETH GOULD

Elizabeth was a talented artist who provided the illustrations for one of Darwin's bestselling books. Her husband John was the highly respected ornithologist who successfully identified many of the bird specimens that Darwin brought back from the voyage.

SIR JOSEPH DALTON HOOKER

Darwin's closest friend and supporter was director of the Royal Botanical Gardens at Kew. He was one of the first scientists to read Darwin's *The Voyage of the* Beagle and urged him to publish *On the Origin of Species*.

DR ROBERT GRANT

Grant gave up medicine to study marine biology and was a major influence on Darwin's development as a scientist. He donated his own collection of specimens to the University of London and these are now on display at the Grant Museum of Zoology

JOHN STEVENS HENSLOW

This Cambridge-based botanist and geologist inspired Darwin and encouraged him to become a naturalist. Henslow turned down the opportunity to sail on the *Beagle* and recommended that Darwin take his place.

THOMAS HUXLEY

In an historic debate on evolution held at the Oxford University Museum in 1860, Huxley supported Darwin's theory against religious critics including Bishop Wilberforce (see next page) and the captain of the *Beagle*. Called 'Darwin's Bulldog' for his reputation as a powerful and tenacious supporter of Darwin and natural selection.

LORD KELVIN

A leading scientist of the time, Lord Kelvin was one of many who disagreed with Darwin's theory. He believed the world was millions of years old rather than billions.

THOMAS ROBERT MALTHUS

Malthus wrote an important book about population growth. Many of his findings remain highly controversial but others influenced Darwin when he came to formulate his evolutionary theory.

JEAN BAPTISTE LAMARCK

A French naturalist whose work was highly influential. Before Darwin was even born, he was a strong believer in evolution but (unlike Darwin) was unable to explain the process by which it occurred.

JOHN MURRAY III

Murray was the publisher of *On the Origin of Species*. The book was reprinted multiple times and in many different languages, and is still in print today. His descendants later sold Darwin's handwritten manuscript to the National Library of Scotland.

CHARLES LYELL

A Scottish geologist contributed to Darwin's ideas about evolutionary theory and was one of several friends who helped arrange the publication of his ground-breaking book.

ALFRED RUSSEL WALLACE

This British naturalist and explorer came up with his own theory of natural selection after visiting the Amazon. It was his decision to publish his ideas that persuaded Darwin to complete *On the Origin of Species* in 1859.

PROFESSOR ADAM SEDGWICK

Cambridge University's Professor of Geology took the young Darwin to Wales to study rock formations in the area. The two became friends but the professor was one of several academics who strongly argued against Darwin's theory of evolution.

BISHOP SAMUEL WILBERFORCE

A popular public speaker whose father campaigned to end slavery in the British Empire, Bishop Wilberforce was one of many churchmen who objected to the idea that Darwin should be knighted by Queen Victoria.

SIR RICHARD OWEN

An English palaeontologist (a fossil expert), Richard Owen invented the word 'dinosaur' and helped Darwin classify many of the specimens he collected on his voyage. Despite this he did not agree with Darwin's theories, which ruined their friendship.

EMMA WEDGWOOD

Darwin married his cousin Emma, the grand-daughter of a rich and famous potter. They had ten children and he hoped she would edit *On the Origin of Species*. Unfortunately, she died before he had finished writing it, but their daughter Henrietta edited some of his later work.

GLOSSARY

Anatomy
The scientific study of body parts.

Archipelago
A group of many scattered islands.

Blasphemy
Disagreeing with or criticising the teachings of the Bible.

Creationism
The belief that God created the universe, the Earth and every living thing in six days, as told in the Bible.

Earthquake
A sudden shaking of the ground caused by movement in the Earth's surface.

Essay
A formal piece of writing putting forward or discussing an argument, theory or opinion.

Evolution
The theory that all kinds of living things developed from earlier types, with changes occurring over millions of years.

Fossilise
The transformation of the remains of a plant or animal into rock or mineral form, preserving them for millions of years.

Genetics
The scientific study of genes, which are what make each living thing unique, and how they vary between generations.

Naturalist
A person who studies plants, animals and other aspects of nature.

Natural selection
The name Charles Darwin gave to the process by which animals and plants become better-suited to their environments over time.

Offspring
The young of an animal or plant.

Specimen
A physical example, living or dead, of a creature, plant or fossil.

Species
A set of animals or plants that do not differ much from each other, meaning they can be studied as a group.

Survival of the fittest
The phrase now used to describe the way that only the animals and plants that are best-suited to their environment will have the chance to reproduce.

Zoology
The scientific study of animals.

TIMELINE

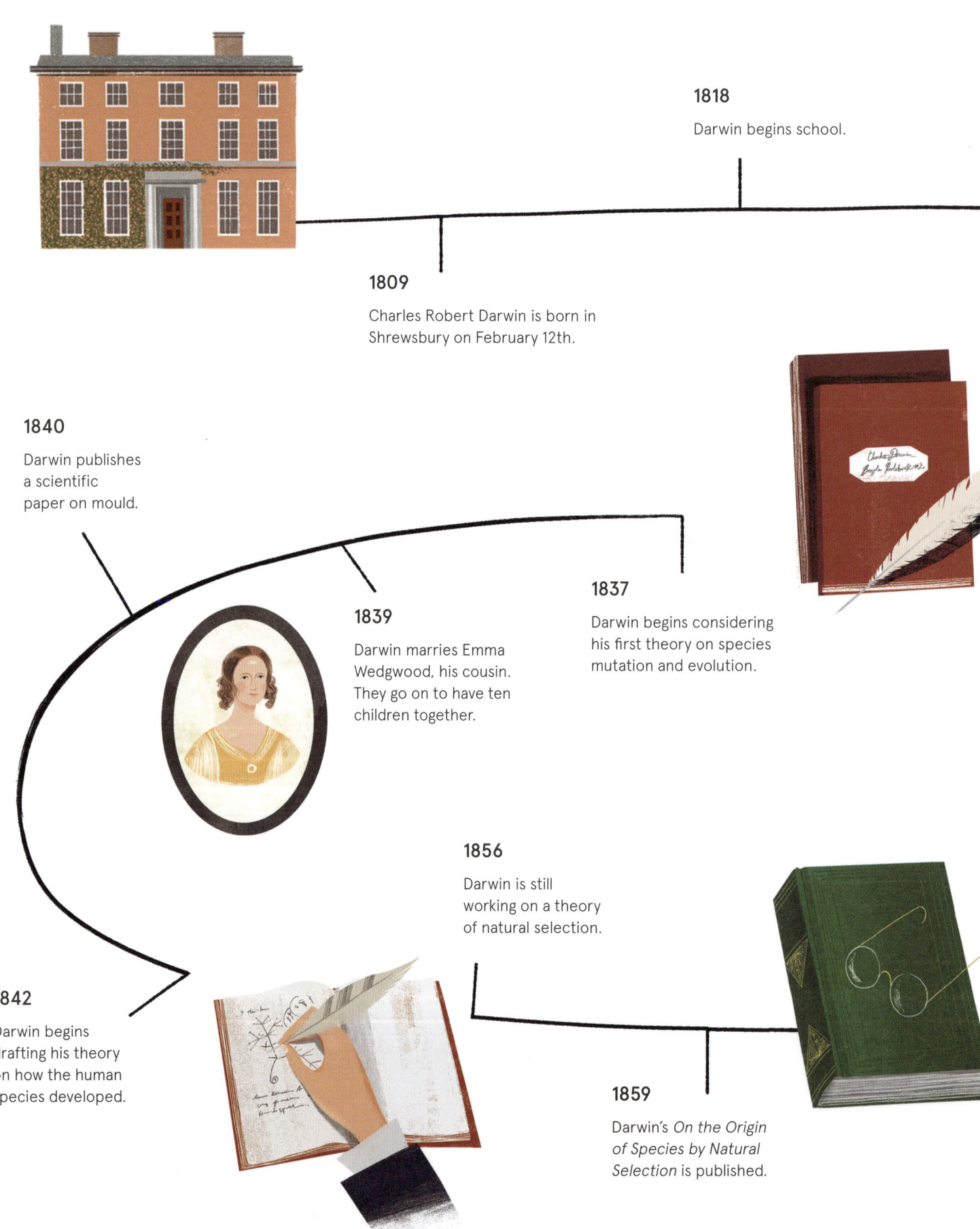

1818
Darwin begins school.

1809
Charles Robert Darwin is born in Shrewsbury on February 12th.

1840
Darwin publishes a scientific paper on mould.

1839
Darwin marries Emma Wedgwood, his cousin. They go on to have ten children together.

1837
Darwin begins considering his first theory on species mutation and evolution.

1856
Darwin is still working on a theory of natural selection.

1842
Darwin begins drafting his theory on how the human species developed.

1859
Darwin's *On the Origin of Species by Natural Selection* is published.

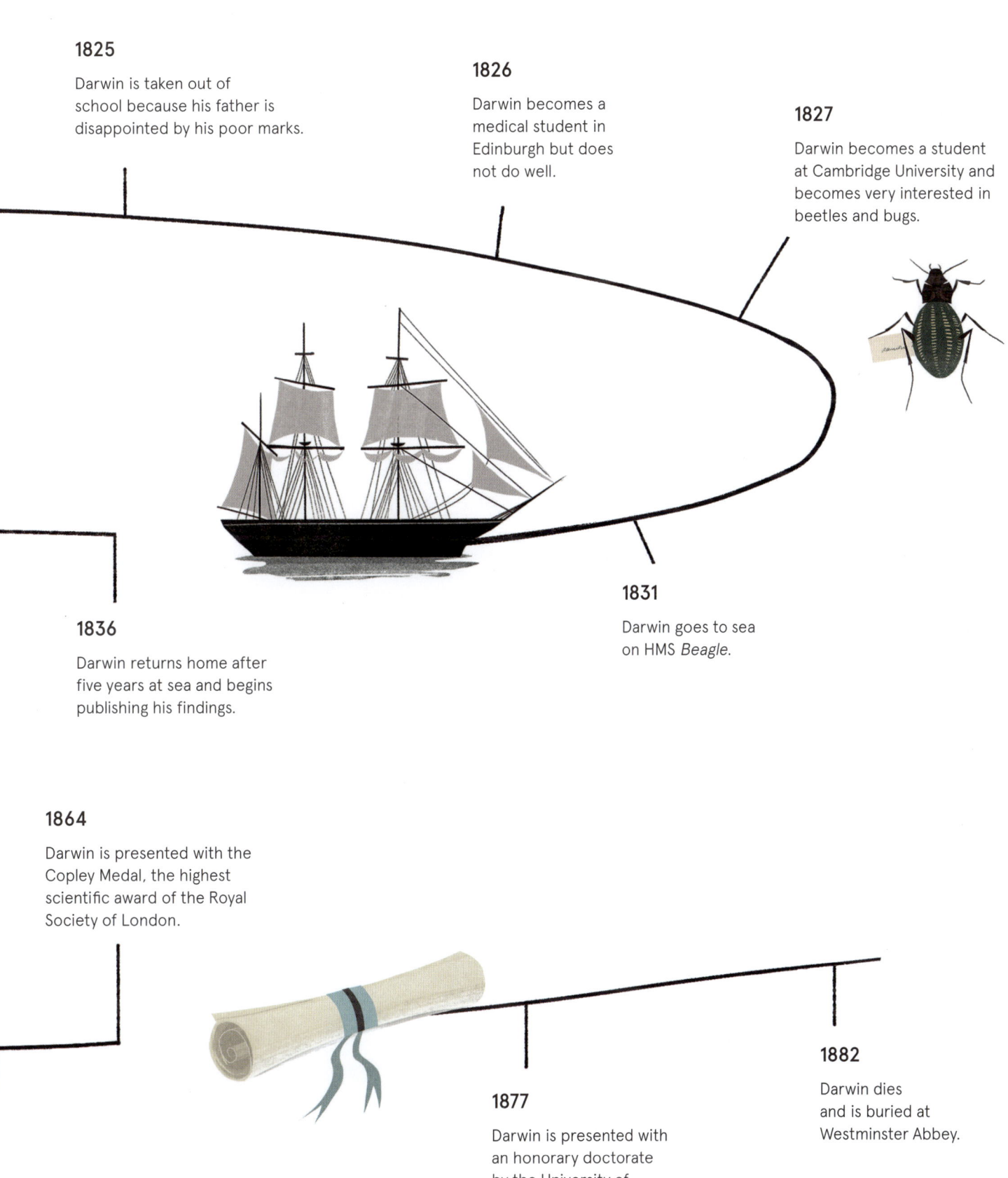

1825

Darwin is taken out of school because his father is disappointed by his poor marks.

1826

Darwin becomes a medical student in Edinburgh but does not do well.

1827

Darwin becomes a student at Cambridge University and becomes very interested in beetles and bugs.

1831

Darwin goes to sea on HMS *Beagle*.

1836

Darwin returns home after five years at sea and begins publishing his findings.

1864

Darwin is presented with the Copley Medal, the highest scientific award of the Royal Society of London.

1877

Darwin is presented with an honorary doctorate by the University of Cambridge.

1882

Darwin dies and is buried at Westminster Abbey.

Inspiring | Educating | Creating | Entertaining

Brimming with creative inspiration, how-to projects, and useful information to enrich your everyday life, Quarto Knows is a favourite destination for those pursuing their interests and passions. Visit our site and dig deeper with our books into your area of interest: Quarto Creates, Quarto Cooks, Quarto Homes, Quarto Lives, Quarto Drives, Quarto Explores, Quarto Gifts, or Quarto Kids.

Text © 2020 David Long. Illustrations © 2020 Sam Kalda.

First published in 2020 by Wide Eyed Editions, an imprint of The Quarto Group. The Old Brewery, 6 Blundell Street, London N7 9BH, United Kingdom. T (0)20 7700 6700 F (0)20 7700 8066 **www.QuartoKnows.com**

A catalogue record for this book is available from the British Library.

ISBN 978-0-7112-4966-0

The illustrations were created digitally

Set in Apercu

Published by Georgia Amson-Bradshow
Designed by Myrto Dimitrakoulia
Edited by Claire Grace
Consultant Niall Sreenan
Production by Dawn Cameron

Manufactured in Guangdong, China TT022019

9 8 7 6 5 4 3 2 1